Bishop Toby's Pilgrimage; or, the Method of procuring a mitre

Anonymous, Henry Bishop of Exeter. Phillpotts

Bishop Toby's Pilgrimage; or, the Method of procuring a mitre, etc. [A satirical poem on H. Phillpotts, Bishop of Exeter.]

Anonymous
British Library, Historical Print Editions
British Library
Phillpotts, Henry Bishop of Exeter.
1832
54 p. ; 8°.
11602.ff.15.(2.)

The BiblioLife Network

This project was made possible in part by the BiblioLife Network (BLN), a project aimed at addressing some of the huge challenges facing book preservationists around the world. The BLN includes libraries, library networks, archives, subject matter experts, online communities and library service providers. We believe every book ever published should be available as a high-quality print reproduction; printed on- demand anywhere in the world. This insures the ongoing accessibility of the content and helps generate sustainable revenue for the libraries and organizations that work to preserve these important materials.

The following book is in the "public domain" and represents an authentic reproduction of the text as printed by the original publisher. While we have attempted to accurately maintain the integrity of the original work, there are sometimes problems with the original book or micro-film from which the books were digitized. This can result in minor errors in reproduction. Possible imperfections include missing and blurred pages, poor pictures, markings and other reproduction issues beyond our control. Because this work is culturally important, we have made it available as part of our commitment to protecting, preserving, and promoting the world's literature.

GUIDE TO FOLD-OUTS, MAPS and OVERSIZED IMAGES

In an online database, page images do not need to conform to the size restrictions found in a printed book. When converting these images back into a printed bound book, the page sizes are standardized in ways that maintain the detail of the original. For large images, such as fold-out maps, the original page image is split into two or more pages.

Guidelines used to determine the split of oversize pages:

• Some images are split vertically; large images require vertical and horizontal splits.
• For horizontal splits, the content is split left to right.
• For vertical splits, the content is split from top to bottom.
• For both vertical and horizontal splits, the image is processed from top left to bottom right.

Bishop Toby's Pilgrimage;

OR,

THE METHOD OF PROCURING A MITRE.

BISHOP TOBY'S

PILGRIMAGE;

OR,

The Method of Procuring a Mitre.

IN SIX STAGES.

NARRATED BY HIMSELF BY WAY OF ADVICE TO HIS SON.

NEWCASTLE:

PRINTED FOR THE AUTHOR, BY W., E., AND R. MITCHELL,
AND MAY BE HAD OF THE BOOKSELLERS.

————

1832.

BISHOP TOBY'S PILGRIMAGE.

STAGE I.

SINCE, Ned, I wish thee to aspire
To pious honours like thy sire,
I now shall point thee out the road
Which I with much success have trod:
Meanwhile thou may'st such hints select,
As may be useful to direct
Thee, in the path of piety,
To wealthy stall and deanery;
And what's much better still and brighter,
The gem of holy gifts,—a mitre!
Let, then, the precepts I impart,
My son, be graved upon thy heart. (1)
   On leaving, while as yet a boy,
The grammar-school, my next employ
(A circumstance I blush to tell)
Was waiting in my sire's hotel. (2)
But I had often heard it said,
As well as seen myself and read,
What reverence and respect were shown
To all the brethren of the gown;
Who, for their weekly sermons, prayers,
And some few minor pastoral cares,
Were wont to get a recompence
Of still more weighty consequence,

A

A splendid list of tithes and fees,
Of fines, fat glebes, and moduses!
And, tho' scarce yet eighteen, my mind
Was then so piously inclined,
That I preferred these sacred things
To ev'n the wealth and pomp of kings;
And every wish and prayer of mine
Was to become a great divine;
To make the Church of Christ my care;
And have, besides, a handsome share
Of those fair gifts so amply given
For cleric use by gracious heaven!
   My father, tho' a publican,
Was always deemed an honest man;
And, like most landlords, was expert,
Nay, happy, in the pleasing art;
Possessed a fund of hum'rous jests
To entertain his jovial guests.
With these, and matchless powers of song,
He oft was wonted to prolong
Their festive mirth for many an hour—
A scheme to swell the drinking score.
But all professions, from the clown
Ascending upwards to the crown,
Not ev'n excepting that of preaching,
Have such like arts of overreaching,
And claim as *lawful* perquisites
Whate'er they *pilfer by these slights!*
I, therefore, did not mean to blame
My sire, because he practised them,
Who, to his *honour* be it said,
Acquired a fortune by his trade!
Howe'er, his cares were such that he
Ne'er gave his mind to piety;
Nor would he sanction the design
I'd formed of being a divine;

But when I such a wish expressed,
He treated it as but a jest—
Was wont to say, with serious air,
He thought his own a better far
Than ev'n the clerical vocation,
Deducting costs for graduation.
But this was all a mere pretence,
Which he contrived to save expense;
For never mortal man was more
Intent on hoarding up his store.

    Thus, by my sire's severe behest,
My pious project was suppressed,
And all my views—O, sad to tell!—
Confined within a curst hotel!
But after all, 'twould be uncivil
To blame my sire—I blame the Devil!
Who doubtless tempted him, good man,
To thwart and counteract my plan,
By plying all his artifice
To fill his mind with avarice,
Lest he, perchance, should give his coin
To aid me in my good design.
For if we scan the sacred pages,
We find, in apostolic ages,
That, often with too much success,
This prince of crime and craftiness
Has fettered with impediments
The good designs of ev'n the saints!
And hence I wonder not that he
Presumed t' enthral a youth like me,
Deeming he'd gain his wicked end
By fettering me—malicious fiend!—
In an hotel to be the slave
Of every coxcomb, sot, or knave,
That in so vile a place might choose
To banquet, revel, and carouse,

On whose commands I had to wait,
From morning soon to evening late,
And for their jeers and insolence
Return the smile of complaisance.
While harassed thus from day to day,
With bustle, noise, and drunken fray,
I scarce could stifle my chagrin,
And cursed, (may heaven forgive my sin!)
Tho' secretly, the clamorous sots,
As well as bottles, pipes, and pots,
Which oft I broke, too, in my wrath,
For standing in preferment's path.
   But while with hopes of heavenly height
I thus was doomed to mourn my fate,
And struggle with ignoble cares,
I had the luck, I thank my stars,
To spend a vacant hour or two,
As I was sometimes wont to do,
In poring o'er the Odyssey ;
And thus I caught a stranger's eye,
Who chanced to be my father's guest,
And what was more, he was possessed
Of affluence, and had a spirit
To patronize a youth of merit,
And since he soon perceived in me
Great classical proficiency,
He tendered willingly his aid
To drag me from my servile trade,
And, as entitled by my lore,
Enrol me 'mong the reverend corps.
His offer I (you well may guess)
Accepted straight with eagerness :
Thus what my frugal sire denied
Was unexpectedly supplied ;
And since he now perceived his purse
Was not to suffer, he of course

Quite willingly assented to
'The holy project I'd in view.—
Thus heaven vouchsafed to rescue me
From thrall of hellish subtlety !
And shortly after with a swell
Of joy I left the curst hotel,
Fully resolved my skill to prove,
In Isis' academic grove!
   I scarce had been a twelvemonth there,
Beneath a reverend tutor's care,
Till I'd the honour to surpass
The first Etonians of my class ;
And bore with ease (I'm proud to say)
The freshmen's classic prize away.
But as to all the cumbrous store
Of ethics, mathematic lore,
And systems founded by a toil
Of Newton, Bacon, Locke, and Boyle,
Such useless lumber I neglected,
And all my power of mind directed
To Burnett, Bentham, Warburton,
To Sherlock, Hoadley, Tennison ;
Who shone with so much brilliancy
In modern church theology,
And won the public approbation,
By wrangle, cant, and disputation ;
And other pious rarities,
Which they "imported from the skies,"
And which, like fashionable wares,
Were sure of meeting purchasers.
   In short, from these profound divines,
I took my maxims and designs ;
Whose subtle arguments I noted,
And in my essays either quoted,
Or, with slight metamorphoses,
Mixed up with my own sophistries,

I passed them off as wholly new,
And that with such assurance, too,.
That all my brethren of the gown,
With wonder struck, agreed to own
My essays peerless specimens!
Nay, ev'n the learned tutors, deans,
Declared they could perceive in me
Such ardent zeal and piety,
Such depth of talent and research,.
As would do honour to the church!
And matched me 'gainst its foes as one
Prepared to be its champion,
And wield its apostolic brand
Against the whole united band
Of infidels and sectaries,
And other baneful enemies;
Who'd most audaciously of late
Begun to vend their spleen and hate
Against our holy church, and brand all
Its sacred institutes with scandal;
And stigmatize, with one accord,
Its faithful servants in the Lord,
As bastard scions of the whore
That dwelt at Babylon of yore.
    It kindled up my holy wrath,
To hear my church's rites and faith
Reproached, confuted, vilified,
By enemies on every side,
And all its gown fraternity
Assailed with such virulency;
While no attempt of consequence
Was made in shape of a defence.
But since my brethren of the college
Had all consented to acknowledge
My talents in theology,
'Twas quite enough t' encourage me

To use those talents to detect
The errors of each modern sect,
And, lo ! I soon became acute,
Both to expose them and confute !
For he who thus could batter down
Another's church, exalts his own,
Secures his brotherhood's regard,
And seldom fails to get preferred—
And now, well armed with subtle wit,
Backed out with texts from holy writ,
I sallied forward to withstand
Th' assaults of this most impious band,
And soon began to make them feel
"The pious ardour of my zeal ;"
Did boldly vindicate withal
My church's creed and ritual ;
And my success in this good cause
Procured me more and more applause.

What I on this occasion wrote,
Tho' now a thing of minor note,
Was reckoned then a dextrous hit
Of subtle argument and wit,
Was long the theme of conversation,
As well as praise and admiration ;
And being but a "junior soph,"
It set my talents highly off !
This, in the pamphleteering trade,
Was the first effort that I made,
But I, of pamphlet scribes the prince,
Have written many a hundred since,
Whereby I've dealt my church's foes
Full many signal overthrows ;
And for my *pious* labours, too,
Have got what richly was my due,
The highest honours of the gown,
As in due order shall be shown.

Since then my rising star had now
Dispelled the clouds that hitherto
Were wont to dim and mistify
My path to cleric dignity.
I persevered with nothing less
Than full assurance of success;
And growing daily more acute
In subtile wrangle and dispute,
And all the train of high church cant,
As well as acting sycophant,
I thus secured a stock of friends
To help me to my pious ends.
'Mong these, a youth of noble line
Was a peculiar friend of mine ;
And what was more, his sire was dead,
This youth his heir, and would succeed,
Soon as he passed the minor's age,
To vast estates, with patronage
Of many a wealthy rectory,
The best of which he promised me !
I made myself this lordling's tool—
For him I pimped and played the fool ! (3)
Indeed, at all the sacrifices
He offered to an hundred vices,
I ministered !—In short, my leisure
I oft devoted to his pleasure !
And that his friendship might not slide,
I left no servile art untried !
I did the same for others, too,
Who had like favours to bestow !
This served by way of relaxation,
Amid the toils of graduation,
And gave me double energy
For studying divinity !
I thus " *did ill that good might come,*"
A maxim disapproved by some—

But I would gladly learn from them
Why they're so hasty to condemn ?
If thus I compass good, no doubt
I'll get reward, at least I ought
To have reward :—it follows, too,
If I make good from ill ensue,
I shall have compassed "*a conversion*,"
On which whoever throws aspersion
Profanely spurns, and sets at naught
What saints in every age have taught—
Et ergo, good I still shall prize,
When ev'n from ill I give it rise!'
An adept in such craft as this,
His *pious* aim will rarely miss ;
For many sprightly youths I've known,
Who now with honour wear the gown,
And made their way, by such devices,
To wealth, to stalls, and benefices,
Who else had never risen high
Among the church fraternity :—
And few, indeed, I'm *proud* to tell,
Could me in such like tact excel !

STAGE II.

In Isis' bowers I now had spent
Four tedious twelvemonths of restraint,
Had duly run the circle o'er
Of *Alma Mater*'s holy lore,
As well as taken my degree
The needful requisite A.B.;

B

And tho' I'd got a stock of knowledge
Adapted to a life at College.
I was determined not t' engage
In stickling for its patronage,
Nor in a fellowship to loiter
In monkish mode, nor be a tutor
To train those dunces, fops, and asses,
That constitute our college classes,
Nor nightly join in the carouses
Of doctors, deans, and heads of houses,
A tribe of stupid formalists,
Of noisy pedants, egotists,
Of rhymsters, rigid devotees,
As well as drones and debauchees,
That merely wear the hallow'd cloth
To shield their follies, vice, and sloth.
Such the discordant elements
That constitute our Oxon saints !
And tho', much like my own, their zeal
Is ardent for the church's weal,
Doubtless the only thing in which
They may be equal to my pitch ;
Yet characters of such a cast
Were ne'er adapted to my taste,
For such is the stupidity
Of academic pedantry !
That one, like me, of buoyant spirit
Could ne'er be reconciled to bear it.
And now quite sick of the delights
Of such like reverend bedlamites,
And trusting that my bland behaviour
And talents had secured the favour
Of many friends quite competent
To free me from this vile restraint,
I now began to fix my eye
On vicarage and rectory,

From whence I could extend my view
To wealthy stalls and mitres too,
And all the pomp and consequence
Attending cleric affluence.
   Thus I, who but four years ago
Was tavern boy obscurely low,
And slave-like doomed to wait on all
Who for my services might call,
Had made my way at such a rate
Among the learned and the great
Of Oxon's gown fraternity,
That to a lordly prelacy
My hopes, ev'n then, were wont to rise,
Which since I've lived to realize.
   With zeal becoming a divine
I kept in view my good design,
And soon found out a nearer way
That in my sphere of action lay
T' accomplish it, than any I
Had in my ardent piety
As yet attempted—for as soon
As I'd got on the holy gown,
And by most solemn inaug'ration
Had entered my divine vocation,
I left the flock, then in my care
As proxy, scattered here and there.;
And bent my amorous skill to prove,
I hastened to the myrtle grove,
Where love-warm Venus keeps her court,
Where sighing nymphs and swains resort,
And lo! among this train I shone
As erst among the sophs I'd done,
While I must own the amorous smile
Of blooming belles possessed a wile
So truly irresistible,
That ev'n in me its subtile spell

Was wont to wake that sinful flame
Which ill becomes divines to name :
But summoning all the energy
Of both my faith and piety,
I thus contrived to guard my heart
Against such fascinating art,
Nor once so far forgot my duty
As e'er to yield to such vain beauty
As wanted those divine perfections—
Rich portions or renowned connexions!
    An heiress to a large estate
Of course I woo'd to be my mate,
Nor spared my wiles and adulation
To win this lady's approbation.
She seemed so void of all deceit,
And with such warmth my flame to meet,
That lo! I formed the proud surmise
That I'd completely won my prize!
But soon I found her so beset
With lordling, 'squire, and baronet,
And flattered by this courtly train
My chosen belle had grown so vain,
So full of jiltish artifice,
And in her choice so very nice,
That soon I found, with deep regret
Her wealth was not so good to get;
As for herself, I cared no more
Than for a tawdry Oxford w—e.
Hence I thought proper to dismiss
All such fallacious hopes of bliss,
And straitway fixed my choice upon
A dame whose hand and heart I won.
As to her beauty and her fortune,
They scarce could make her worth my courting ;
But she secured my approbation
Because she had a great relation

To help me to a benefice;
For she'd the luck to be the niece
Of England's then Lord Chancellor, (4)
And shortly afterwards I bore
To Hymen's fane my sighing dove,
To consummate our plighted love!
   By this huge stride at once I found
My foot on rich preferment's ground,
Which gave my heaven-directed hope
A field of more extended scope,
And brighter prospects—I, in short,
Had now procured " a friend at court."
Indeed my *pious* hopes aspire
On friendship's score but one step higher,
I mean the friendship all good men
In hallowed courts above obtain,
Tho' we may reach these blest abodes
By more obscure—tho' smoother—roads,
Less devious, and, of course, more short
Than that which leads thro' William's court;
Still I this grand highway prefer.
Meanwhile I must confess that where
The mitred gifts of heaven are found,
Temptations far the most abound,
Which lead, in spite of zeal and faith,
Some pilgrims from the heavenward path.
However, I trust, I can't get wrong,
My zeal and faith are both so strong—
So strong as to surpass by far
What mostly fall to mortal's share.
Not long I waited after this
Till I procured a benefice,
The Chancellor, now my relative,
To me, good christian, deign'd to give
A vicarage on the banks of Tees, (5)
And that, too, in the best of sees—

The envied see of Durham, where
Such wealthy stalls and rectories are ;
Altho', meanwhile, I must confess,
The step I just had made was less,
Much less, indeed, by far, than what
My lofty hopes were driving at.
While I, in courtesy, was now
Forbid, at least a year or two,
To press the Chancellor, my friend,
His bounty further to extend ;
But since I'd talents of a cast
That hardly well could be surpassed,
Should but an opportunity
Occur to show their energy,
And thus to catch (a hopeful plan)
The glance of my diocesan,
I made no doubt I soon would rise
In this rich field of enterprise.
And this I wished the more to do,
Since 't would be adding to my bow
Another string, to swell the score
Of those I had obtained before.
 The duties of my cure meanwhile
I stickled in with *seeming* toil,
Exhorted my parishioners
To be attentive to their prayers,
And feigned most deep solicitude
For all their souls' eternal good,
As well as temp'ral happiness.
Indeed I could not well do less
For sake of cleric decency,
And the repute I'd gain thereby ;
For such would bear a good report
Unto my lord the bishop's court,
As well as if I'd done the whole
With all my energy of soul.

I, pushing on designs like these,
Took the commission of the peace;
And now my mind was wholly bent
On studying acts of parliament—
All this I did with a pretence
To save my worthy flock expense,
As well as trouble and vexation
Attending distant litigation,
By settling at my house their jars,
Their rate—and turnpike road—affairs
But I had nobler ends in view
Than wasting time o'er such a crew!
Or reconciling reprobates
For breaking one another's pates!
For know, in secret my design
Was, Tully-like, to make a shine
Among the Durham magistrates
In sessions—and assize—debates,
In which I gained no small applause
For depth of judg'ment in the laws.
This led me ostentatiously
Into first-rate society,
Which, by the way, is a position
Becoming clerical ambition.
And if the world produce such parsons,
(Tho' such I deem are very scarce ones,)
As are " to all their country dear,
And rich on forty pounds a year,"
That always watch and pray with rigour,
Nor make in polished life a figure,
I wish them from my heart success,
But envy not their happiness;
For when I took the priest's commission,
It was no part of my ambition
To spend a life of drudgery
In curate-like obscurity ;—

No, no, I still the maxim hold,
So much revered in days of old
By many a truly good divine,
That piety's more genuine,
Shines more conspicuous and brighter,
When robed in sleeves of lawn and mitre,
Than it can ever do when dressed
In humble garb of parish priest ;
Tho' modern sects maliciously
Attempt to prove the contrary,
Whose wicked cant is meant no doubt
To sink the church's fair repute.
 Surely these brawlers ne'er have hit
On what a holy father writ,
Whose name and nation I've forgot,
Howe'er I can the passage quote :
" *A good work* truly he desires
Who to the deacon's post aspires,
He who desires to wear a mitre
Desires *a better*," says this writer ;
He says " *a better*," but I say
The best when I include *the pay*,
For every man requires regard
Proportioned to his post's reward.
 This doctrine, too, comes very nigh
What Paul held forth to Timothy, (6)
In verse the first of chapter third,
A text the best upon record ;
Pointing direct to "*a good work*,"
That now employs his Grace at York ;
And that "*good work*" was just the same
To which I bent my *pious* aim.
 But notwithstanding all my care
To gain my point, for many a year
I had to wait without success,
Till now I thought it time to press

My relative, the Chancellor,
Complaining that my stall was poor,
To whom I set its value forth
At less than half its real worth!
  I sent to my diocesan
A controversial specimen,
Wherein I'd played my sophistries
Against his lordship's enemies—
I mean the liberals and the whigs,
The sectaries and their colleagues,
And strove to gain a presentation,
With all my power and adulation.
  To forward this my good intent,
Epistles, too, I often sent
To the young lord, the friend I made
At college, as already said.
I wrote him, in my humorous style,
Some Durham joke, to make him smile;
And dwelt upon our pranks and frays
At Oxford, in our youthful days—
Reminded him, just at the *finis*,
His promises were standing *minus*.
But these three lords, yea, all the three,
My idols, then, and trinity,
In spite of all my *pious* care,
Refused to listen to my prayer;
While I, chagrined most grievously,
Beheld their favours passing by!
I hope the Trinity above
Won't be so cool, and hard to move,
When I with equal zeal implore
Their favour at " the trying hour!"
It makes me pause to think of this,
But I shall now these thoughts dismiss,
And if high heaven should grant my will,
I shall defer such thoughts until

My mitre-hunting pilgrimage,
And all its cares, cease to engage :
I'll then be quite at liberty
To think of heaven more seriously,
Hoping my present avocation
Will meet its highest approbation.

STAGE III.

One day, while lounging in my chair,
My mind engrossed with holy care—
That is to say, intent upon
How stalls and mitres might be won ;
And viewing, too, in retrospect,
How I'd been treated with neglect,
And left upon a paltry living,
Scarce worth the trouble of receiving,
To spend my time, and talents, too,
Among a groveling rustic crew,
On whom my skill, as a divine,
Was thrown away, like pearls to swine—
I could not help but vent my spleen
Against the conduct of those men
On whose professions I relied,
And stickled for so long beside,
By carnal wile, or holy shift,
Just as their humours seemed to drift,
From whom, of course, I hoped ere this
To get a wealthy benefice ;
Nor thought they'd treat such piety
As mine with scorn and contumely.

Chagrined that such should be my fate,
I sunk, almost disconsolate,
Into a paroxysm of grief;
When, lo! to give me some relief,
A stock of pamphlets came to hand,
Which gave me soon to understand
My good diocesan, Old ———, (7)
Had got into a hot dispute
With those arch fiends, the jesuits,
Who had declared his church's rites
And holy faith unscriptural,
Most spurious and schismatical;
I found, too, that they'd nearly floor'd
With arguments the mitred lord,
While all the priests from Tweed to Tees,
His lordship's dronish protegees,
The most of whom were daily living
Upon the bounty of his giving,
And who in duty should have made
Strong efforts in their patron's aid,
Neglected him at such a crisis,
Nor strove to thwart the foe's devices,
Contrived the church to undermine,
But careless slumber'd on supine,
Or wallowing deep in gluttony
And manifold debauchery!
But what can any one expect
From such like drones but base neglect!
Who merely seek fat benefices
T' indulge their indolence and vices!
But I, a needy aspirant,
Well armed with quibblery and cant,
And all befitting sophistries
For such a pious enterprize,
As well as eager to be made
The leader of a new crusade,

And that against the self-same foe
On which I wished my strength to show,
Rushed forth and took the bishop's side,
And his exulting foe defied;
And to repel the calumnies,
The foul-mouthed and audacious lies,
And other vile aspersions, thrown
With Jesuitic rancour on
Melancthon, Luther, and on all
That rid the church from popish thrall.
I straight assailed those miscreants,
The Piuses and Innocents,
The Bonifaces, Gregories,
The Leos, Johns, and Sixtuses.
And all that filled the papal chair,
And searching out with special care
The records of their bloody deeds,
Their impious rites and pseudo-creeds,
I soon presented to my foes
A list of blacker acts than those
Which they, with all their deep research
Could muster to impune my church.
The papal claim infallibility,
I treated, too, with such scurility
And vile contempt, as well became
The arrogance of such a claim;
While they in their defence inferred,
If by such claim their church had erred,
My church would certainly be found
In error on the self-same ground,
Since it monopolized salvation
By acts of test and corporation,
Which put (I could not this disown)
All other sects and churches down,
Which was assuming a degree
Of self-sufficient purity,

That in effect it might as well
Have claimed to be infallible!
   For this I made a good defence
By urging the " expedience"
Of such infallibility
When but admitted *tacitly*,
But still maintain'd the papist err'd
When such they *openly* declared.
Strong proofs of this may be adduced
That should not publicly be used,
For every church is wont to drive at
Important pious ends in private ;
For instance, grasping more and more
Of riches, dignity, and power,
Till even kings themselves shall be
Subservient to the hierarchy !
When thus a race of faithful pastors
Rule those whom men call lords and masters
They next may, for the church's good,
Make all submit to servitude,
And yield their goods and consciences
Into their hands as their trustees,
Of which, on getting full possession,
They may dispose at their discretion.
   A lordly stretch of power thus gained
May be as piously maintained,
By punishing the disobedient
Not as a church—but state—expedient !
These things divines should ne'er reveal
If they've at heart their church's weal,
For were they openly declared
'Twould put mankind upon their guard,
And make them hesitate to give
The church its due prerogative.
   Thus being shackled with restraints
As to my choice of arguments,

I only galled my enemies
By playing off my sophistries ;
At length the jesuits, wheeling round,
Took what they deemed commanding ground,
And straight assail'd with bitterness
Our good reforming Queen, old Bess,
While I attacked her sister Mary ;
As to their sire, our eighth King Harry,
Nor they nor I thought fit to claim him—
Of course we both agreed to damn him :
They to exalt their church's glory
Doomed him to endless purgatory,
While I, with equal zeal for mine,
Did straight to hell the wretch consign.
   They next, with great asperity,
Upbraided with apostacy
Our bishops Cranmer, Latimer,
And many a shining character,
That claim both praise and admiration
For bringing round the reformation,
For whom, as such, I made defence
With all my powers of eloquence.
I hurled the brand, too, of dishonour,
At Wolsey, Gardiner, Pole, and Bonner,
And many a mitred pseudo-saint
That figured off at Nice and Trent,
And many a jesuitic bigot
That wholesale dealt in fire and faggot,
In confiscation, massacre,
Indulgences, and such like ware !
   I now supposed my foes' defeat
Was most decisively complete,
But lo ! the subtile jesuits wheel'd,
And took once more another field.
Their rancour now was dealt on Knox,
The champion of Scotch orthodox,

As well as every *pious* deed
His followers did beyond the Tweed :
On this I fell, with equal heat, on
The wicked acts of Cardinal Beaton,
And many more as black as these
Done by his Scotch accomplices,
From which I drew a counter list,
And paid them back with interest!
   Long thus both pure and spurious saints
Produced us themes for arguments,
Whom we assaulted or defended
Just as our faiths and interests tended,
And roughly canvass'd o'er their deeds,
As well as doctrines, rites, and creeds,
Until we made most thorough searches
For all the glories of our churches,
Nor spared our virulence and cant
To prove that if the world would grant,
To us divines, that stretch of power
Which we possessed in days of yore,
We ne'er would have our minds perplex'd
With searching Scripture for a text
To prove our faith and doctrine by,
And maul the sons of heresy,
But still as erst adopt the sword
As stronger than Jehovah's word!
   We many a lengthy pamphlet lined
With vigorous efforts of this kind,
At length my popish enemies,
Confounded by my sophistries,
Confessed themselves discomfited,
And straightway turned their backs and fled.
Thus boldly did I fight, as saith
The Apostle, " *the good fight of faith,*"
And as by heaven's appointment Gideon
O'ercame the wicked host of Midian,

So I was destined to o'ercome
The modern Dagonites of Rome.
But if I'd choose, (my tact is such,)
I doubtless could have done as much
In favour of the popish party,
But I, indeed, could ne'er be hearty
In such a cause, when I perceive
They've no rich benefice to give
In recompence for genuine
And ardent piety like *mine*.

Thus having borne the bishop out,
And put our common foe to route,
I gained the ends I had in view,
His lordship's praise and favour too,
Who, to reward my piety,
Soon gave me a rich rectory, (8)
Made me his chaplain, and in short
The prime director of his court,
Which I must own was a position
That highly flattered my ambition,
For now my brethren of the gown
Feared worse than hell my pious frown,
Who all by gifts and bland behaviour
Began to stickle for my favour,
As the most likely way t' engage
His lordship's envied patronage.
My wife, too, on the same account
Got presents to a large amount,
As well as great supplies of toys
For all her little girls and boys.
Such were the arts employed to bribe
My favour by the reverend tribe.

Just as I hoped, this lucky step
Proved the precursor to a leap,
For next, what to my lot did fall
I got a rich prebendal stall!

I still as erst kept whirling back
The insults of the audacious pack
Of papists, whigs, and sectaries,
My lord the bishop's enemies,
In which, by way of pamphleteering
And stickling at electioneering,
I always met with such success
As pleased my patron more or less.
Meanwhile it was my wont to ply
The mitred lord with flattery,
(In which, I trow, I far excelled
My great precursor, Chesterfield,)
Which was with such effect employed,
That when his Weardale stall was void (9)
I had the great felicity
To have the prize presented me;
Than which no bishop that I know
Could a more splendid gift bestow,
And in my hands, with little trouble
I soon found means to make it double;
For know, I am surpassed by few
In searching out a latent due,
Or adding to my tithing score
Ev'n such as ne'er were paid before.
My Weardale sheep, poor silly flock,
Know well that this is not a joke—
That on the heathy mountains there
Were scattered oft for lack of care,
Just once a year I penned them in,
And fleeced them to the very skin;
And as the faithful servant whom
His lord left agent when from home,
Who did one single pound receive,
But when his lord returned had five,
So was the pound my lord gave me
Improved by proper agency,

D

Till now 'twas five—but five of what?
Of thousands sterling!—mark ye that!
For such was now my annual pay!
Thus I fulfilled, I'm bold to say,
Most faithfully what heaven commends,
As well as gain'd my private ends.

At length my patron, worn with years
And pious apostolic cares,
Exchanged for a celestial crown
His earthly mitre—and as soon
As heaven accomplished this design,
The clergy of his palatine,
With one accord, agreed to raise
A sculptured tablet to his praise.
And what did all this reverend tribe?
They called upon me to subscribe!
And tho' I knew my brethren would
Upbraid me with ingratitude,
I deemed it proper to discard (10)
Their silly whim! for what reward
Could I expect if I should rear,
With costly toil, a sepulchre?
Could I expect to be repaid
For such like trouble by the dead?
Away with such an idle whim!
I now could get no more from him!
And taking Scripture for my guide,
I find it still upon my side,
For what is such a bootless deed
But "*leaning on a broken reed.*"

STAGE IV.

———

Since on preferment's heaven-ward road
I made so far my journey good
As to have got " *in medias res*,"
Nought less than deaneries and sees
Were in my *pious* wishes now,
I took of course a wider view
As to the distance and the height
To which I next could wing my flight,
And oft, indeed, my thoughts would carry
Me ev'n as far as Canterbury.:
But should I fail to reach so far,
My aim was York or Winchester.
For seeing greater feats were done
By Wolsey, a poor butcher's son;
By Sixtus, who'd once scarce a home,
But died the papal lord of Rome;
By Beckett, too, and many others
Enrolled among the saints their brothers,;
These bright examples of success
Impelled me on with eagerness,
To make attempts at emulation
In this my reverend avocation,
And fired my mind with holy zeal
For my immaculate church's weal!
   The impulse of paternal love
Besides was often wont to move
My ardour in this good design,
For now my wife had brought me nine
Most hopeful sons, and daughters five,
(A swarm sufficient for a hive,)

"And her ambition and my own
" Was that our sons should wear the gown."
Of course I could not well do less
Than wish to rule a diocese,
And thus possess the patronage
Of rectory, stall, and vicarage,
And have within my reach at once
The means of settling all my sons,
As well as have it in my power
To hoard my daughters each a dower;
I'd friends and relatives beside
For whom I thus wished to provide;
As for myself I then would stand
Among the nobles of the land,
Invested with the dignity
Attached to a prelacy,
Which, added to the joy it gives
To aggrandize one's relatives,
Must be, as I would calculate,
Approaching near that blissful state
Which heaven beyond the tomb designs
For all good orthodox divines.
   To help me to my *pious* end
I now employed my powerful friend
The Chancellor ;—besides, I wrote
A pamphlet, which his lordship thought
A grand attempt in vindication
Of th' acts of his administration ;
And furthermore I praised his zeal
For our most holy church's weal,
And our most sacred constitution
As settled at the revolution—
A noble Gothic fabric, such
As cannot be admired too much :
I stigmatized most loudly, too,
The ever brawling whiggish crew

As reprobates and innovators,
Rebellious demogogues and traitors:
All this I then could do *sans* fear,
But times are changed, opinions veer,
For then their power was very low—
I wish it had continued so.

   For what I wrote on this occasion,
As well as being his relation,
The Chancellor kindly promised me,
Good christian, the first vacant see !
The promise of this saintly prize
O'erpowered my mind with extacies,
Such was my joy to think I'd get
What I'd so long been aiming at,
While none in conscience could, I trow,
Deny a mitre was my due.
Indeed, my fame was now so high
For faith-defending chivalry,
That all good churchmen every where
My name were wonted to revere,
As one that wielded Gideon's sword
'Gainst the blasphemers of the Lord ;
Besides, my having the support
Of such a powerful friend at court,
Gave every person to foresee
Such interest and *such* piety
Would soon command a prize no lighter,
'Twixt saints and sinners, than a mitre.

   But soon, alas ! it grieved me sore,
My friend and his colleagues in power
Thro' dotage, death, and want of talent,
(Which last has long been deemed a small want,
Nor tending to depreciate
A minister of church or state,)
The charge of court affairs gave up,
And thus o'erthrew my lofty hope !

Misfortunes seldom come alone,
For while I now was woe begone
And fainting from this fatal stroke,
It gave me still a rougher shock
When Canning, noisy advocate
Of modern whims in church and state
And catholic emancipation,
Became the premier of the nation,
And worse than all, took for colleagues
My most inveterate foes the whigs,
And those, besides, the very men
On whom so oft I'd shewed my spleen,
Because I knew they did not care
How ill our holy church might fare ;
Hence, nothing I could now expect
But to be treated with neglect :
Besides, I feared 'twould be my lot
To lose what I'd already got,
If such an innovating band
Should sway the destinies of the land.
    My mind, inflamed with holy wrath,
As well as steadfast in the faith,
I set to work with all my might
To arraign their measures wrong or right,
But chiefly bent my energy
Against religious liberty,
And other schemes of reformation
With which they agitate the nation,
Which any one may well foresee
Will tend to crush the hierarchy,
And throw dishonour on the gown,
If not successfully put down,
And should in duty be withstood
By all who prize the church's good.
    These things I clearly pointed out
In various pamphlets which I wrote,

Insinuating that the whigs
Were aiming, by their vile intrigues,
At nothing less than to restore
The popish miscreants to power,
And called the clergy to unite
To shield the church with all their might,
Nor spare their efforts to oppose
And dissipate their whiggish foes.
　　This false alarm had an effect
As good as I could well expect,
For hosts of staunch high-church divines
Soon joined me in these good designs,
Who having made a truce with routes
And other such like gay pursuits,
Or shaken off, tho' somewhat loath,
Their favourite companion sloth,
On whose soft couch some priests indulge
More than 'tis proper to divulge,
From which, indeed, they ne'er awake
Except their interest be at stake,
And seeing now, with rueful face,
That this was like to be the case,
Came forth t' avert the impending skaith
And aid me to defend their faith ;
Or what amounts to just the same,
To vindicate their sacred claim
To tithes, fat glebes, and moduses,
And other such good things as these ;
For know divines are wont to feel
In this good cause a fiery zeal—
So fiery as to shed the blood
Of those by whom it is withstood :
For many proofs of this, go search
The annals of our holy church.
　　Now that the onset might be made,
Of this our anti-whig crusade,

With such decorum as became
Our hallowed apostolic aim,
I marshalled all my pious host,
Assigned to each his proper post,
As Michael in high heaven's domain
Did erst his pure angelic train,
And from our pulpits every where
We blew the trump of holy war,
Proclaimed the Anti-christ of Rome
Had hitherward resolved to come,
And that he'd made most solemn leagues
With both the devil and the whigs,
That in defiance of the Lord
This impious band with fire and sword
Had vowed to vent their hellish wrath
On all that held the christian faith ;
While pamphlet, placard, and gazette,
Were duly used to propagate
This false alarm, until they bore
Its awful sound from shore to shore.
All this was every where believed
Soon as the tidings were received.
(O credulous, happy ignorance !
Thro' thee we priests have still a chance
To hold those honours, wealth and power,
Thou gav'st so bounteously of yore.)
Thus soon we raised the good old cry
"*No Popery!!! No Popery!!!*"
" *The church in danger*" thro' the crowd
Was bellowed, too, both long and loud.
Thus soon we kindled up a train
Of fears and terrors false and vain,
As well as rage and enmity
Against the whiggish ministry ;
And this we did, with such success,
That in a year—nay, somewhat less,

Our foes, the whigs, I'm proud to tell!
Perceived their posts untenable,
And straight resign'd their high command
Into my friend Duke Arthur's hand,
The staunch and steady advocate
Of Gothic forms in church and state,
And all things termed legitimate:
I need but mention Waterloo
To prove him pink of heroes too.
 I having by this *holy* shift
Contrived to set the whigs adrift,
Had now the joy to see the tories
Exalted to their former glories,
And my dear church released once more
From dreaded thrall of whiggish power;
While I, as champion of its cause,
Was introduced, with great applause,
At court, which raised my expectation
Ev'n to a prouder exaltation
Than ever it attained before
Thro' favour of the Chancellor;
For I was certain that my friends,
Because I'd help'd them to their ends,
Would never think to offer less
Than place me o'er a diocese.
But O how treacherous and how vain
Are ev'n the hopes of pious men!
For all they thought of giving me (11)
Was but a paltry deanery!
This gift is but a kind of step (12)
O'er which I've oft seen parsons leap,
And know my strength of faith was such
That I designed to do as much;
But since 't has been my fate to use it,
It ill becomes me to abuse it,

Seeing it helps one on one's way
To Durham, York, *et cetera*.
  I now shall close another stage
Of this my holy pilgrimage,
And if, meanwhile, I'd got my due,
I'd had a mitre on my brow.

STAGE V.

  Scarce had my friends the Duke and Peel,
For both the state and church's weal,
As well as for their own and their's,
Assumed the charge of court affairs,
When, lo! the impious popish clan,
Led on by noisy lawyer Dan,
And other demagogues of Erin,
Began to make such loud careering,
Excite such tumults and sedition,
And set the Duke, too, at derison,
That now he found—O, sad to tell!—
Their claim quite irresistible
To Catholic Emancipation.
Of course the Duke's administration
Gave up their efforts to resist
These panders of the Anti-christ,
And openly espoused their cause,
The same which I with such applause
Resisted not so long before,
And, Gideon-like, proved conqueror.
  What part I'd take in this affair
Was matter for the premier's care,

For know, he dreaded seriously
My pamphleteering battery,
Which long had dealt such fatal skaith
Among the sons of popish faith,
Would now be used to countermine
His present cabinet design!
  I kept aloof meanwhile, and made
Remarks on what was done and said,
That I more acc'rately might learn
How matters by and by would turn,
In order that I might direct
My prowess to the best effect
To gain my pious purposes,
Of which the leading three are these :—
Firstly, to keep the spoil I'd won,—
Second, to get a lawn-sleeved gown,—
Thirdly and lastly, to oppose,
If there was need, my popish foes.
As to the last, I soon, indeed,
Perceived that there was urgent need:
However, for a mitre's sake
I deigned another course to take,
For scarcely had I drawn my pen
To vent my swelling wrath and spleen
'Gainst all the hosts of Anti-christ,
As well as boldly to resist
Th' intentions of the cabinet
By means of pamphlet and gazette,
And thus arouse the church divines
Once more to second these designs ;
When, lo ! I had the great good luck
To get a letter from the Duke,
Inviting me to come to court.
I, therefore, cutting matters short,
Straight ordered out my coach—got dressed—
Set off to learn the Duke's behest,

And when I reached his Grace's house
I supped with both himself and spouse—
No, I mistake, I ought to say
His Grace had turned his spouse away,
(For marriage is but meant to bind
The lower orders of mankind,)
And her he'd now was but his harlot,
I recollect her dress was scarlet,
And that she smiled with gracious mien
Whene'er she looked on me, the dean ;
In truth she was a peerless beauty,
Enough to make me slur my duty.
As for the Duke, he squeezed my hand,
Was highly complaisant and bland,
While he and his dear paramour
Used all the efforts in their power
To wheedle me to second them
In their emancipating scheme.
And what was more, they promised me
The gift of the first vacant see,
With choice of future favour, too,
If I would swallow all the spew
And nasty filth I'd vomitted
Both on the living and the dead,
And tongue-lick clean both these and those
Whom I'd bespattered as my foes,
And afterwards their cause defend
As I would do for any friend.
    This trial, you'll agree, was hard,
But seeing such a great reward,
I just had half resolved to do it,
But paused awhile, ere I set to it,
To search a proper vindication
For my designed tergiversation,
And was successful in my search,
For, lo ! the fathers of the church,

As well as apostolic saints,
Hold forth unnumbered precedents
Of having changed their rites and creeds
And these extolled as pious deeds.
Just one of weighty consequence
I shall produce in my defence.
St. Paul, with enmity deep rooted,
The church of Christ once persecuted,
And hurled upon it rage and terror;
But soon as he was shown his error,
With equal zeal he advocated
The self-same church he spurned and hated.
This great apostle has besides
Such deeds still further justified,
For in Corinthians, says he,
" *All things are lawful unto me,*"
From which 'tis plain the saint implies
That we may veer and temporize
When such is found " *expedient,*"
As well as done with *good* intent.
    Thus, in my conscience justified,
I skulked o'er to the popish side
Quite unawares, and left my church
And all my brethren in the lurch.
But soon as the report was spread
That I their champion now was fled—
That I the church's firmest stay
Beyond all hope had given way,
Both friends and foes—O, sad to tell!—
(This plot was surely hatched in hell!)
Uniting straight upbraided me
With baseness and apostacy—
Most loudly both by writ and word;
But such the servants of the Lord

Have oft, 'tis known, been doomed to feel,
Ev'n when they sought, with warmest zeal,
Their own, their church, and country's weal,
And which I did on this occasion.
Of course I bore the castigation
With pious christian fortitude,
Seeing my motives were so good ;
But heaven by such like trials proves (13)
The faith and zeal of those it loves.

Howe'er, my conscience still resists
The papists, *alias* Anti-christs,
Altho' it cannot be denied
I've trucked and stickled on their side ;
That is to say, my mind and deed
Can be at variance when there's need.
As when a bishop first receives
The lordly mitre and lawn sleeves,
He mutters "*nolo episcopari*"—
Mark how his tongue and heart can vary,
His very action kicks his word,
And this is sanctioned by the Lord,
As all the saints agree—and why
Need it be doubted ?—they'll not lie!
Besides, 'tis done and always should
With a design of doing good,
And such was my design when I
In act, *not* thought, backed popery,
Which drew upon me so much hate.
Howe'er, to ease its grievous weight,
The premier Arthur still remained
My patron, favourite, and friend,
Who deigned to take me for his guide, (14)
And by my council to decide
On matters of important weight
Respecting both the church and state ;

And I advised him to repeal
(A thing I never must reveal)
The acts of test and corporation,
Tho' 'twas against my inclination,
And that because it took away
From my dear church another stay.
But I'd no way save this whereby
To whirl my secret enmity
Against the priests, especially those
Who had of late become my foes.
  I'd scarce been thus engaged two years
T' assist the Duke in court affairs,
Until it pleased him to prefer
Me to the see of ————.
Thus have I got, with much ado,
The prize that long has been my due,
And tho' it be a lordly stall,
Plague on it, still my pay is small!
However, now I take my stand
Among the grandees of the land,
A rank to which my piety
So properly entitles me!
While like a king I hold my court,
To which whole tribes of priests resort,
From whom large offerings I receive
Of what I've long been wont to give,
I mean the incense adulation!
Why?—'cause I've got the presentation
To vicarage and rectory,
To which they cast a wistful eye.
But spite of all their flattery,
Their high pretence to piety,
And all their other holy shifts,
The best of these, my cleric gifts,
I shall bestow upon my sons,
Pray God they all were fit for gowns!

My nephews and my near relations
Come next in turn for presentations,
The most of whom I fear may be
Not blest with my ability
To raise themselves in church or state;
But those disqualified by fate
For gaining great and noble ends
Stand most in need of powerful friends!
And 'tis my maxim to dispose
Of such inactive wights as those,
By wrapping them in cleric gowns
And sending them to preach to clowns,
Where none are able to descry
Their want of good ability,
Where practising a few restraints
They'll be revered and pass for saints,
Will get their tithes, and fines, and fees,
And live in affluence and ease:
For there are drones in every hive
That on its richest nectar thrive.

Among the various blessings given
To him who, by the grace of heaven,
Has got a mitre, there's one more
Which I forgot to name before.
If he have daughters, heaven provides
Most graciously to make them brides; (15)
For know, the cleric bachelor eyes
A bishop's daughter as a prize,
Feels always happy to resign
His heart into her charms divine,
He then becomes a bishop's son
And then his pious end is won;
That is to say, a step like this
Will raise him to a benefice!

Indeed, 'twas part of my design,
And well becoming a divine,

To win my girls this privilege
When I to bishoprics laid siege,
So great was my paternal love,
Which God and man alike approve.

STAGE VI.

I now have reached the final stage
Of this my holy pilgrimage:
Besides, I've got, in some degree,
Rewarded for my piety.—
Doubtless the Duke had raised me up
Ev'n to the acmé of my hope
Ere this—had not the foul intrigues
Of his detested foes the whigs,
And whom I've every cause to hate,
Deprived him of the helm of state;
Who drove both him and me from court,
And cut our expectations short,
  While I was vexed with this affair,
The Weardale sheep, then in my care,
Were led astray by a huge ram, (16)
And when I strove to gather them,
This ram with such ferocity
Presum'd to butt and bound at me,
And thus, beyond all parallel,
Made ev'n my harmless sheep rebel;
That, to my sorrow be it told,
He spurned and drove me from the fold.
These wicked pranks made glorious sport
For all my whiggish foes at court,

Who backed the efforts of the brute,
And laugh'd to see him drive me out,
And draw the sheep out of my care—
I'll ne'er forget this sad affair!
Sure never was received by pastor
From his own flock such dire disaster!
As to this ram, pray God the beast
May make some ravening wolf a feast!

Thus did I lose my wealthy stall,
(How I am doomed, alas! to fall!)
The stall which Arthur pledged to be
Held *in commendam* with my see ;
While I with sorrow and dismay
Behold my ancient foe, Lord Grey,
In full possession of the post
My noble friend Duke Arthur lost,
And Grey has called his clamorous band
From all the corners of the land,
Who, spite of all my subtile art
And pamphleteering schemes to thwart
Their doubtless-sacrilegious aim,
Began with all their force to frame
A threat'ning battery, "*the Bill*"
Misnamed "*Reform,*" (confound their skill!)
To crush, demolish, and erase
My holy church's firmest stays—
I mean the boroughs which I doat on, (17)
Which lying whigs denounce as "rotten:"
But I persist these stays are good,
Else how could e'er the church have stood,

But I'd the joy (I'm proud to say !)
To get revenge on whiggish Grey,
For all the gross indignity
He and his crew have heaped on me ;
For when he'd reared his lofty fort,
And laboured hard a twelvemonth o'er't,

And was about to seal the fate
Of all that's great in church and state,
Our hero Arthur sternly rose,
Resolved to check his boasting foes,
Who, with his veteran tory band
In squadrons well appointed, and
The mitred phalanx of the Lord,
Uniting all with one accord,
Rush'd boldly forth, and took by storm
Their threat'ning stronghold of reform!
And thus he sav'd Old Sarum, Gatton,
And all the burghs by whigs called " rotten."
But common sense this charge denies!
(The whigs are fam'd for telling lies;)
Indeed, I hold these burghs to be
The soundest props of liberty,
And hop'd to stay the church they'd stand
The *pride and glory* of the land,
And that by their assistance I
Would rise to mitred dignity,
And that e'en to as high a pitch
As saintly Beckett's self did reach.—
But, lo! beyond my expectation
I had the sorrow and vexation
To see Lord Grey and his colleagues
Rally their wicked band of whigs,
Who straight with all their might began
To renovate on a new plan
Their threatening battery once more!
But ere they'd got their works mature,
My mitred brotherhood and I
Employed our utmost energy
T' excite commotions and divisions,
By means of pamphlets and petitions,
Among the panders of reform,
Spreading abroad a false alarm,

That Grey with all his whiggish list
Had leagued themselves with Anti-christ,
And warning all good protestants
To shun such wicked miscreants,
Who had, for certain, a design
The christian faith to undermine.
But we were left, alas! to grieve
That none would these reports believe!
I blame "the march of intellect"
For bringing round this bad effect,
Seeing we'd thus success before
When Canningites aspir'd to power.
 Since nothing thus could be effected,
We all our chosen friends collected,
Resolv'd to try our former course,
That is, t' employ an open force,
And straight, with Arthur at our head,
We press'd the fort by escalade,
And thus against the Broughams and Greys
We wrestled hard for full four days,
But found, (it grieves me much to tell,)
Our whiggish foes invincible!
 Howe'er, we did not still despair
Of some success in this affair;
For seeing, as we'd erst design'd,
Their stronghold might be undermin'd—
Indeed, the Duke himself agreed
This was most likely to succeed;
And he and Tory Lyndhurst straight
Set to the work with all their might,
And sapped their strongest bastion wall,
While Grey, foreseeing it would fall,
With all his innovating host,
In haste resolved to quit his post.
This gave me ample hopes once more
To see my patron rais'd to power;

And soon he got old Grey's commission,
Altho' it was on this condition,
To rear again what Grey design'd,
The fort he just had undermin'd!
And carry on the reformation
So much against his inclination!
And crown once more his honours by
Political apostacy!
And since no better could be done,
I would have gladly helped him on;
But, lo! the panders of reform
Began to raise so rough a storm
Of rage and tumult thro' the land,
That none of Arthur's trusty band,
Not even Hardinge, Peel, and Baring,
Were found so headstrong and so daring
As join his Grace on this occasion;—
Of course, I had the dire vexation
To see Lord Grey and all his train
Resume their former posts again!
Tho' I was wont to watch and pray
Most fervently, both night and day,
That Heaven might graciously prevent
So unpropitious an event;
But spite of every art of mine,
Grey has accomplished his design,
Has made a thorough revolution
In our most sacred constitution,
By forcing out its Cornish props,
In which I always placed my hopes,
And substituting such like ware
As Halifax and Manchester.
　　Howe'er, the Duke, myself, and ours,
Have still, I trust, sufficient powers
To spurn the Russells, Broughams, and Greys,
And shield the church in after days;

Nor do I even now despair
Of reaching York or Winchester.
In one or other of such stalls,
· Had I not got so many falls,
I'd been ere this—but I may blame
The whigs, and that rude Weardale ram :
A gang of vile, rebellious traitors !
As well as impious innovators !
They've dealt me many a ruthless stroke,
And many a dangerous stumbling-block
They've cast before me, to delay
My journey on my heavenward way!
And if they dar'd attempt the deed,
Would knock the mitre off my head !
They'll be rewarded by the Lord
According to their deed and word !

   Howe'er, my son, spite of the bustle
And enmity of Grey and Russell,
I've got a see, with patronage
Of rectory, stall, and vicarage,
And other holy gifts, whereby
I can reward thy piety,
And give thy consequence a pitch
Beyond what once I hop'd to reach,
And free thee thus from many a care
That in my youth fell to my share.

   I've told thee now my pilgrimage,
From pot-boy youth to mitred age ;
At least I think I've touched upon
My noblest deed : from which, my son,
I hope thou'rt able to deduce
Examples for thy future use.
And in addition to all this,
I think, dear Ned, 'twont be amiss
To read some ten or twenty score
Of my best tracts and pamphlets o'er,

By which I raised my humble name
Supreme in theologic fame.
And since divines of this our day
Regard them as Apocrypha;
In after times, no doubt at all,
They'll be esteemed canonical!
Besides, I'd have thee to peruse,
And enter deep into the views
Of the renown'd Lord Chesterfield;
In whose epistles is reveal'd,
With great acuteness and precision,
How men should act in every station,
As well as how to gain their ends
Of such as call themselves their friends.
And now, my son, if thou wouldst thrive,
And by the world respected live,
As well as be hereafter blest,
Mark, learn, and inwardly digest
The rules I've laid so clearly down,
To both thy honour and my own!

END OF THE POEM.

NOTES.

Note 1, page 3.

" Let then the precepts I impart,
My son, be graved upon thy heart."

" My son, forget not my law," &c.
PROV., c. III., v. 1.

Note 2, (ibid.)

" My next employ
(A circumstance I blush to tell)
Was waiting in my sire's hotel."

The Bishop of ~~Exeter~~ was, at the beginning of his career, a pot-boy in his father's inn at ~~Bristol~~, a city in the west of England ; from whose conduct and character, as a stickler for church-preferment and a pamphleteering controversialist, " the subject matter" of this pilgrimage is principally drawn.

Note 3, page 10.

" I made myself this lordling's tool,
For him I pimp'd and played the fool."

It is pretty well known that many young gentlemen intended for the church, while at college, pander to the worst passions of those of their fellow-students who may some day have it in their power either to help them to, or give them church-preferment.

Note 4, page 15.

" For she'd the luck to be the niece
Of England's then Lord Chancellor."

The bishop's rib is said to be a niece of the lady of a certain ex-Lord Chancellor.

G

Note 5, page 15.

" A vicarage on the banks of Tees,
    And that, too, in the best of sees."

B———— M————— vicarage, worth about £200. per
annum, by far too small a sum to satisfy Toby's avarice.

Note 6, page 18.

" This doctrine, too, comes very nigh
    What Paul held forth to Timothy."

" This is a true saying, if a man desire the office of a
bishop he desireth a good work."

1st TIMOTHY, c. III, v. 1.

Note 7, page 21.

" My good diocesan, Old ————,
    Had got into a hot dispute."

This was a controversy between Bishop S———— and Dr.
L————, in which the Bishop in all probability had been
defeated, had he not been seconded by Toby, who displayed,
on this occasion, such an amazing talent of abuse, and that,
too, so much to the satisfaction of the Bishop, that he made
him his chaplain, and gave him the choice of his preferment
as it became vacant !

Note 8, page 26.

" Who, to reward my piety,
    Soon gave me a rich rectory."

G———— Rectory, worth between £1,000. and £2,-
000. *per annum.*

Note 9, page 27.

" That when his Weardale stall was void," &c. &c.

S———— Rectory, which, when presented to Toby,
was reckoned to be worth £3,000. per annum, but which
he soon increased to £5,000. and upwards, by means of
rigorous exactions, not only of the customary tithes, but also
by imposing tithes on potatoes, turnips, &c., &c., which had
never been previously paid.

Note 10, page 28.

" I deemed it proper to discard
    Their silly whim."

It is a fact that Toby, after having received so many and
great favours from Bishop S————, (his late diocesan,)

actually refused to contribute towards the expense of erecting a monument to his memory.

Note, 11, page 35.

" For all they thought of giving me
Was but a paltry deanery."

The Deanry of C———, in the west of England.

Note 12, (ibid.),

" This gift is but a kind of step
O'er which I've oft seen parsons leap."

Many clergymen are made bishops without having previously been deans.

Note 13, page 40.

" But heaven by such like trials proves," &c.

" For whom the Lord loveth he correcteth," &c.
Prov. c. III, v. 12.

Note 14, (ibid.).

"Who deigned to take me for his guide."

It is pretty well known that Toby was the prime director of the duke's councils during his premiership.

Note 15, page 42.

" If he have daughters, heaven provides
Most graciously to make them brides."

It is well known that bishops' daughters are eagerly sought after by the " amorous cleric bachelor" with a view to preferment.

Note 16, page 43.

" The Weardale sheep then in my care
Were led astray by a huge ram."

Mr R——— of S——— Castle is here allegorically represented as "a huge ram," who, when Toby was promoted to the see of ———, called a meeting of the inhabitants of S——— parish (Toby's " sheep,") at which a petition was drawn up and sent to Mr Peel, the then Home Secretary, demanding a resident rector, and remonstrating strongly against the S——— living being made a sinecure to gratify episcopal avarice; the S——— Rectory having

54

been designed to be held *in commendam* with the see of
———— by our hero Toby, which design was thus frustrated.

Note 17, page 44.

" My holy church's firmest stay—
I mean the boroughs."

Our *ultra* tories and orthodox churchmen, it is well known, consider the nomination, or more properly *rotten* boroughs, the *soundest* part of the constitution."

ERRATA.

Page 8 line 18, for " vend," read " vent."
— 18 — 23, for " requires," read " acquires."
— 26 — 35, supply the *note of interrogation* at the end of the line.
— 38 — 29, for " This trial, you'll agree, was hard," read " This task, I can't but say, was " hard."
— 40 — 22, for " all the saints," read " modern saints."
— 45 — 20, for " to," read " in."

THE END.

o

W., E., and H. Mitchell, Printers, Newcastle.

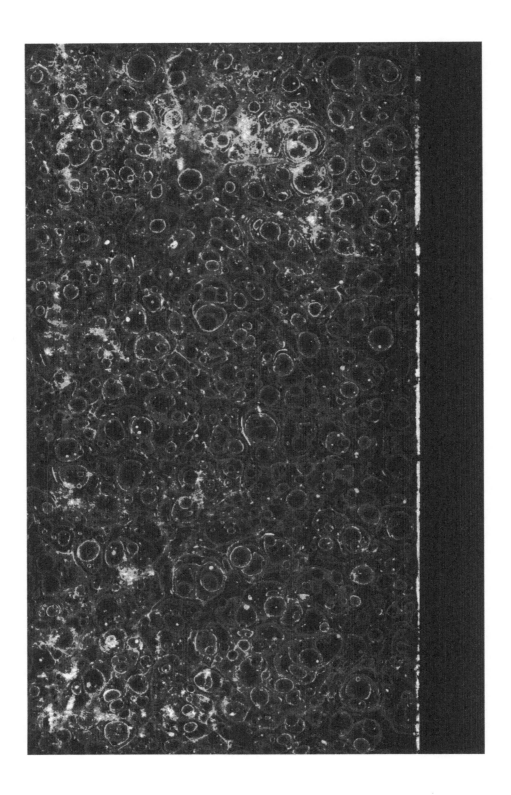

Lightning Source UK Ltd.
Milton Keynes UK
UKOW07f1904090815

256649UK00009B/158/P

9 781241 170004